The Easter Story

Published in Nashville, Tennessee, by Oliver-Nelson Books, a
division of Thomas Nelson, Inc., Publishers, and distributed in
Canada by Lawson Falle, Ltd., Cambridge, Ontario.

Printed in Malaysia

Library of Congress Cataloging-in-Publication Data

Pipe, Rhona.
The Easter story/Rhona Pipe; illustrated by Annabel Spencely.
p. cm. — (Now I can read Bible stories)
Summary: A simple retelling of how Mary Magdalene discovered the
empty tomb and saw Jesus alive after his crucifixion.
ISBN 0-8407-3420-4
1. Jesus Christ — Resurrection — Juvenile literature. 2. Mary
Magdalene, Saint — Juvenile literature. 3. Bible stories, English —
N.T. [1. Jesus Christ — Resurrection. 2. Bible stories — N.T.]
I. Spencely, Annabel. ill. II. Title. III. Series.
BT481.P56 1992
232.9′7 — dc20
92-13325
CIP
AC

1 2 3 4 5 6 — 98 97 96 95 94 93

The Easter Story

Rhona Pipe

Illustrated by
Annabel Spenceley

THOMAS NELSON PUBLISHERS
Nashville

"Oh, no!" Mary of Magdala said
to her two friends.
"We forgot about that stone
in front of the cave.
It is too big for us to move.
What will we do?"

Jesus had died three days ago.
It was Sunday morning.
The sun was rising.
Mary and her friends had come
to the garden.
They had sweet oils to rub on
Jesus' dead body.
But now they were stuck.

But wait a minute …
"Look!" Mary said.
"The stone has been moved!
Now what has happened?"
The three friends crept to the tomb.
They went into the black mouth
of the cave.

A young man sat on the stone shelf.

He wore bright white clothes.

The women stood still.

They were too scared to speak.

"Do not be scared," the man said.
"Jesus is not here. He is alive.
Look. His body is gone.
Go and tell His friends."
Mary thought he was lying.
She thought the man had taken
Jesus' body.
She did not know the man
was an angel.

Mary raced out of the garden.
She ran to Peter and John.
"They have taken Jesus' body,"
she said.
"We do not know where it is."
Peter and John ran to the cave.

Slowly Mary went back.

No one was there.

She stood outside the cave.

She cried.

She bent down and looked in.

Two men were in the cave.

"Why are you crying?"
they asked.
"They have taken Jesus' body,"
she said.
Just then there was a noise
behind her.

She turned around.
A man stood in the garden.
"Why are you crying?"
he asked.
"Who are you looking for?"
Mary thought he was the gardener.
She said, "If you took the body, sir,
please tell me.
I will go and get it."

The man said, "Mary!"
His voice was full of love.
Only one man said Mary's name
that way.
Jesus! It was Jesus.
Alive.
"My Teacher!" Mary said.
She was very, very happy.
"Tell all My friends," Jesus said.